THIRTY-SEVEN POEMS:

ONE NIGHT STANZAS

ROB PATTON

THIRTY-SEVEN POEMS:

ONE NIGHT STANZAS

ROB PATTON

an Ithaca House book

Ithaca

Some of these poems originally appeared in
IMAGE, THE TROJAN HORSE, INTRO 3, ed.
by R. V. Cassill, copyright, 1970, by Bantam
Books, Inc. Several of the poems have been
issued first in broadsheet form.

cover photography by Thom Burton

ITHACA HOUSE, 314 FOREST HOME DRIVE
ITHACA, NEW YORK 14850

CONTENTS

for Sarah

THE MANEUVERS

all of the mist
like the small bullets
all separate
and coming fast
different
of differ-
ent rifles
screaming
from the bore
and all of these
these thoughts
unwanted
my mind
leaping from
trench to trench
all unseen
to no avail
they all wound

POEM

a speck of cake on your lip
completes a part of a smile.
what is destined for the next
instant is controlled by
a self-conscious arbitrator
who sees all hints of danger
in my address like one
who divines bad news
from leaves of the tea.
the moment after next
all time follows in parade.
message man you say tartly
your media is my message.
and in the next moment
i may ask you to wipe your
face before we can go on.

RAIN POEM

a storm at five fifteen
and tired breath
of a disused
order of things.
you of all people
run for shelter
in buildings and
their statements
in concrete are
presented as hostile
demands non-negotiable
received after great
anticipation from
the hands of mute
ambassadors.
for me the task
of just taking
the toll of what
has gone down inked
as the mutables
of a history.

RUSH ODE
for Peter Silag

bitter lemons - cool limes
he considered himself an
individualist but he
only expressed it by wearing
socks of odd colors.
can you understand what
is being said under
water? spume surf white
caps waves words
sour grapes - golden apples
christ the first time
when my body got taken by
surprise only now I know.
you should have stopped trying
a long time ago as I
did now whatever comes
and certainly as if what is
real were labeled by an expert.
cry cry cry cry
his socks were two for a quarter
and never washed cry cry

you have been wasting your
life up to this very minute
the other minute after getting
off the waste seemed to shine
gentle and greenish soft-lit
the waste seemed hope no
cry in the empty streets.
The dawn was colored by
an artist of little talent
a kid who had gotten too high
so the brain boiled the kid
the artist the early workers
the classical sun fires up dawn
more streets than people
their morning is my week
their day is what I watch
cry and hope for their night
is still my day until I can
stop it meaning what another
voice of another person from in-
side you reading nietzsche
or holding your hand like
a very young happy girl on a
date inside you cry
a lot it's good for you.

COUNTERS

burned all records,
said they're burned.
double-checked all
other sources and
no lovers were left,
with a kiss in the night,
only left. and Wheeling
and Detroit wept
alone. no one could
call for comfort now,
all the waste in cordial
tidings we say lost.
Paradise Lost.   .   .
de temps perdu.   .   .
the communion of saints.   .   .
the forgiveness of sins.   .   .
next the life ever.   .   .
all
auld acquaintances suffer
from lapse of memory.

the face maybe, the
name I don't know,
they say as they strain
the bottoms of their pockets
for a reply and
the end, they declare
the end is all up to
us.   .   .

COMMUNICATION ARTS

cast your lot among the immortals
I ran over a small dog
getting here to see you
my eyes are just slightly
swollen with easy sentiment

and words are easy and
all the rest is so much
easier with ease it goes
in and so it goes out

in the shadows of the playground
three kids are gathered
to bury it with more ceremony
than they will ever understand

you nearly fell off the bed
but I had to change the record
and voices in a ritual grove
of microphones as dark as

don't cry no more followed by
don't cry no more

I am telling you now that
a cigarette needs a match
the streets outside until I go
home need a friend so
whatever gods you seek to
jilt and men to run bleakly
deranged with rifles and saints
to work their beads over day
and night and dont cry no
more   baby

DEAR EMILY DICKINSON

Dear emily dickinson,
if you only knew
if you only could know
like the lonely-hearts pages
advice and answers:
replies written in lipstick,
problems of tears.
and if you only knew others
beyond the dimming self
and realize that i slither
between clean sheets alone
sleeping with neither
bodies nor beatifications.
nor am i told
what the trouble is
why we are alone in crowds
why total disorder increases,
(horrors neat prim emily)
disorder increases and fragments
alone beget fragments alone

as everything breaks apart
with kind of a giggle,
sparks shatter into others
and we are more alone.
you in your casket
i in my stuttering rocker
baby in the cradle
more alone each instant.
and despairing men
to whom death comes,
shrieking stalks of men
weaving blindly dumbly queerly
and most of all alone
between those tides.
and you emily frightened
reach for your fly swatter
dear emily dickinson
if you only could know.

ORIENTALE

easy.
against all my better
judgement
i speak straight away.
the joints of my bones
crack
on stretching
and it has been weeks
since i have known fear.
if this were the last
day i had
i would go quietly
without heir or love.
but tonight tells me
of tomorrow already.

worked in the shadows
remembered death wears its
victory and a challenge
for all comers. no thoughts
of kindness in close pursuit
of the winter

nor currents of blood
cells and plasma
to cease for the sloth
of the season.

a liking for things
the way they are.
careful responses now
drop out like boxer's
severed teeth. the
coyness which covered
our lives leaves with
the snow. the savage
mind is held within or
underneath.
recognize it for
what it is.

departed.

DREAM OF THREE NIGHTS

for three nights
I have waited for you here
by the bandshell in the park.
each night the musicians,
with false mustaches,
and clip-on ear-rings,
and colorful clothes of Romany
would tune their instruments for me.

I doubt that the weather will hold.
I doubt the gypsy legends
of the stars.
I doubt that you are coming.
Even their fortune tellers
say that you may be a month.

DEAD ON ARRIVAL

either uncovered span or ditch.
starling never move south.
either gratelight or fanned
beginning movement of all bodies
into one clearly damned house.
the need for intrusion and
smiles wasting away right
before the razorbacked hills.
safe as though buried and
forgotten movement through air
or water lost and unknown
to sentries and guards in the night.
if one stirs or bird or creature
whispers then all is as if it was never
begun.

FIRE SIGN WOMAN

In flight I noticed
With fear still hung and plastered in my mind,
The pallor of her small face.
Twilight at noon.
The trembling advancing in great steps.
All greys and greens.

But viewed more objectively,
All things in place,
Facts collected, collated and lists complete,
The substance that had been so real,
Melted as paraffin casing.
Dusk into forenoon.

As a gesture of friendship, someone offered
to mediate.

Meaning in the words,
But the lines that cross the conclusion.   .   .
Never mind her hair, the color of banked fires
Before an economy-crippling strike.
Never mind the facial color
That painters have used for death.
Nor the empty treasuries,
Nor the escape of a few patriots through
                              sewers.

We all end at her feet.

APPROXIMATIONS

jeezsus
how do you choose
to deny
in the worst possible
way
all not given
in literal words
as if they were diamonds
on a green felt
table
of Antwerp

the cutters
and we all could be
cutters baby
are admiring the lustre
and munching luncheon
rolls

then again
one short man
puts one or two
on a pan
of the balances
then another on the
other

JERKING OFF IN JERSEY CITY

kept separate by the flats
(in the multiple sense
of the word) landscape
architecture asphyxiates
the toe hold i have
on the sweaty holy flesh
of your foot.

for a beginning then
all the wasted little selfs
are like strung out junkies
on the worthless streets
of my bed.

all the aimless motion
of their tired ass little tails.
and your sex's suburbia:
verdant world undiscovered.

DIRTY OLD SEPTEMBER

like a solemn honor guard
our offerings into stone
our thoughts into glass
broken as they climb in
the window half the tidings
we said were forsaken
have returned crises in
disguises black beasts rising
out of our loam mind
a candle body a terrorist
torch set into the gravel
to move again the cons say
folly the pros say yes we
will make it but the mist
cast a final vote of no

FIRST POEM

Like movie film running backwards
young men going forward not in but out of
car doors.
Desperate retreats nearly catching one's
      breath.
Ah, lips so firm, red like sliced oranges
unpainted orange and never yet unsliced.
O Laurel I love you, Laurel my love
as I fall out not into your waiting arms.

LIFE IN THESE UNITED STATES

no one talks about decadence
any more you're supposed
to take it into your mouth and
work it around with your tongue
and people can get happy
yeah much less describe it

you have the mind of a slaves
they used to say in the thirties
when they kicked someone out
of their progressive socialist
cell meetings and I very wise
know just when to act for

as my powdered master calls me
for me to come to his starch-
stiff bed and only action will
do I can think of homilies
such as a chain is but strong-
est as its weakest link

the quality of life we offer is
on the whole good oh well
the wages are nil and the tenure
while not eternal is lifelong
take it or leave it you kicking
little sparrow you know
you have one choice

CONVERSATIONS WITH YOU

nothing matters very much
the chance that wallows far
away and can't know his entrance
cue of when to rise from the mire
of earth to birth and when
to make the change for life.

very much no not very much

you scarcely feel it any more
only a slight tremble of the lips
bouncing the words down a rocky
road and only a too quick movement
                    of the hands trying
to retrieve a lost cigarette.

matters no nothing really

was discussed anymore than is
ever said dull pleasantries
meant from the heart what we
really said that pulled cables
between us now forgotten unsaid and
lying, waiting in another country.

after a while our chance gets up
and noses truffles in the loam
what we have had he will not find
all our holdings are in words
memento moris not quite yet
but returned to personal disuse.

1

one, with improbable casings
dark and soft (though metal
to be sure) those piles of star-
shells, ordnance for forgotten
wars. two, is for your
cement tidings delivered
in person. three, the building
itself very solid, the watchman,
old as the last gunhand, punches
in at every hour, just to be sure.
as is living here, as in my dreams,
or your dreams,
or your lover's dreams
you tell me of on mornings when we
have coffee together. what we tell
each other. . . and four, you say
rehearsals are no longer important
just try to sleep, the rest will come
to be. five, it is noon when i
walk along the street.

AGE OF REASON

"Foul 'em up first, we'll reason later!"

picking and repicking at the scabbed
                                    wound.
which is the way that it's always been
done. and where philosophers went
mad sterilely viewing grey german
cityscapes, the scraps of truth
we are sure of could or will be
mean coppers disposed of at
whatever the cost.   .   .
to think about it is madness
worse yet probably fatal.
loose talk never hurt everyone
just about though and the same
glow in the eyes of police making
a long hoped for (an instant at
least an eternity at best) arrest,
the kind it can be shown as coals
existing under certain burning
soils peat or decomposed leaves.
that blaze we feel in our eyes too
we call for action to compensate.

READY NOW

ready now.
my suggested course
of action
is being followed
as you leave town.
each morning
as i brush snow
from my car
i think abstractedly
of distances.
not so much
the one between us
but of their
plurality on the land-
scape. we are more.
they are more
than between two
points.

THE WAYS

slow in deliverance
the frozen ways about me
have never come to form,
less come to age
and something stands wanting
opening the door and want-
ing more than my head,
or my hair, or my shoulders,
and only I can put it off.

once there were two ways about me.
if one was a knifing sort
the other seemed more
and was the favorite
of my choosing . . .

PARABOLA

the chances of even a curve are remote.

anything more direct is out of the question.

what we are faced with
is a different past
than we had thought we had.

broken in by history
our behavioral gelding can only
begin to conceive the race.

but running is worse than
losing.

time is short.

the circle may yet close.

THE HOURS

the hours seem long episodes
of hawkers crying out in torrid
marketplaces at mid-day.
rings for our women. as buyers
we complain of saddle sores and
sand in our traveling costumes.
bolts of cloth wander out into
the landscape. the sun be-
trays the hour for heavy after-
noon sleep. the bath is promised
but never ready until late.
the fruit is always opening
under its own ripeness and
silver is ultimate or in converse
love is tested by hard men's teeth.
skillful precision before marketing.
the stillness of an answer.
any answer or your answer.

ORIENTAL MODE

the mornings are kept short by rising late.
the snows blow in from the west.
knowledge of them eases sleep.
the days go on errands
and are quick to return.
a stiff knot across the back betrays age.
by late afternoon
sunlight is refracted
through an unwashed window
and a glass of beer.
tonight at least
there is nothing to be sorry for.
no one is to be sorry to.

CHOICE WAS

. . . the only access to the road
was narrow and well rocked.
If only I were,
and if only the dangling fears
were to fall,
like half-true rotten fruit
or the foolish children of cliff-dwellers.
The present beginning in
the middle like surgery starting
from the heart, or words retched
up from the stomach, or like a road
that had no meaning to most.
Mostly those who didn't travel
it well and among those even. . .
If only I were
beginning again, and fears
taken in hindsight being
whores once tempting now spent,
shot, overworked flesh, gone or going
wandering far from town on the only
road whose access was narrow.
. . . begin, write, lights glow far away.
If only I were, were. . . narrow. . .

ONE SUNDAY

the quasi haze
at midmorning
the world around
has awakened and
in his sleep he has
missed the connection

the nights were blue
sparks with red embroidery
of live tissue being
poisoned into life

it becomes important
paramount to shake
the pursuers to triple
lock the door to beware
of the air shaft for they
can move through
trapped air as others. . .
quite slowly the sun sets
blacker than ever before.

AFTER WHITMAN

I

The roads are not summers
There is no truth upon them.
The waking from the sleep,
Rubbing one's eyes to watch,
And then cars spearing across;
I am not anxious to talk of this nation,
What interests me is the travel
Which waves the mind into shadow.
As you move to stop and move again
You never think of metaphors
To describe telephone poles.

II

My life is a summer,
My voice is a celebration,
My body is a chamber of commerce.
There is nothing left to expect.

III

Let me tell you how I stood
By the highway waiting for the move.
Then I would tumble into
Then out of automobiles
Not thinking about where they traveled
And only where they stopped
Never secret nor obscure in my
        thoughts
Of buried geography. . . .

THE OTHER THUNDER

the slow ever slowing
seconds
and their message
more true than thunder
the light dim
the sound quiet
and these times
events their placement
sure real all words
that we thought
thunder had meant
when you hear it
near and at night

THE VIEWS

the views from windows more distracting
his coffee like an ever-vinyl fluid
he sits down at his writing table.

the precision of his intentions felt by
all things that meet his eye and crisply
frozen into immutable language just
as fast as he could record. even
below surfaces poetics of souls yes
inanimate souls no challenge maybe.

maybe if you tell little and
then the good hiding you can
give to winds will be restrained.
show me the corpuscles in your ink.
god she said oh my god
the plasmas of my tears wait
too long to thicken. . .

she speaks meaningfully while
he converses in symbols keyed
to a dark profession. her
words today her body tonight
replies to her spun at cyclotron
velocities to remembrances
                    long forgotten.

THE LETTER

Together they read the letter
in the aged lines of light
in the gabled attic dormer.
". . .in any event of my death,"
it said, "the blame is to be affixed
on the betrayers of the word.
Like black vultures they peck
at the meat of my skull."
He hardly knew where to turn,
to his wife or to the window.
The winter-bare elm branches
knew nothing of answers and
she, blowing dust from attic furniture,
never had been fond of puzzles.

1964

Tom Joad, Jr. was wept out
Sitting on a curb of Mill Road East
Wondering over all before him
The Middle America jungle stream.
That morning when we drove to work
We saw him and how we searched
For emotions we never found
In our Swiss cheese sandwiches.
America was at menopause now,
Didn't he know this about her?
So we had to rise up to chase
The rat bastard out of our lives
But he got away into the fields
Wherever night was day. . . .

LAST TO LEAVE

Waiting on with the sense of errors
she had produced like conjuror's cards,
disturbing only the most easily disturbed,
then like a reading of the taroc spread
out to lay a claim on her destiny.

The magic lay in her birth, blood-
warm face kindled by the new air.
The deception came in her growing,
the contact with men and women
seen in the hollows of her hands.

But then the final illusion, the one
which we paid our money for and
commanded to elude our eyes, that one
we only realize after she is gone.

So where I have gone to lengths:
images of the occult do not relate,
as I (long afterwards) spent for breath,
blink away at her changes in fancy.

SPIRO AGONISTES

WASHINGTON D C:
even the haze
squeals on them, stool
pigeons are
rapt with attention,
ears attuned
at wasted words.
definition: hope, verb
of archaic
usage.

rather a suggestion,
choose our product,
hardly quality,
everyone
even suffers: the
key is marketing
statistics
fated by bears
on the exchange.
realize that

seldom in our nation's
peace has
it been more
requisite to
opt for war.

ONE NIGHT STANZAS

I

what black cardiac
arresting all but one of the chambers
breath now nearly without meaning
a piece of work for the coroners
that we are

II

i prayed for the rain
to fall late in december
lightning to burn the snow fields
at least one revivalist to proclaim the
        kingdom of hell
you to be forced near me
in my bed's sanctuary

III

further the plan involved
no leavetaking
the scenario called for angle shots
from storm stained cumulus clouds

IV

the small droplets of spittle on
    cooling lips
the examining physician is reminded
    of SLICKER
a lip product that the television was
    describing
in words and music
as he pulled on his coat
to enter the december storm
to follow roads on call

SOLSTICE TO THE VERNAL

wintry tales and hollow in our orbited
feelings general towards one another,
greater sagas to pass the time
between our lips and when we kiss.

this is a sure and momentous one
which we had better not neglect,
the echo of news bulletins and
the shadows of the stars now northern.

what is best then is this warmth
can you get it? astrologers can claim
this sun for their own as we leave fire,
wounded of the bow, now the goatsmen
amidst to stir trouble, don't you worry.

if this is all I can do is mouth meals
of legends, spill out myths like marbles
from a bag, entertain, be oh so clever,
but not a chance of even this to amuse.

wintry tales, not a teller in sight
no two ears like yours to listen or
body to comfort or fulfill or even
enough sun-light (back to that
at any rate) to nourish the green
wishes I had: brown stalks all
made up in my bed for winter.

THE BANQUET YEARS

you came in to see me
for you had heard music playing
beauty was not stillborn yet
but a gentle fecund swell
a hopeful bulge of younger years.

events had stayed (in the executioner's
sense of the word) in order.

my own peace was still an open hand
yet joyless then and now.
the sham of words whispered to one an -
        other
over pillows indicate this to me.

if by a twist of time or cosmic
reality one time could have been
another and you had come to
hear the music before the phono-
graph or youth or hope (I mean
these words not like those you
whisper now) et cetera were in hock
I mean if you had come to see me
before the music stopped.

SIGNED CONFESSION

you know i am here
by mistake
one of us should be
at our purge trial
midway through hearing
our treasons read
the curious of the capital
pressed for a look
at the guilt in our eyes
but today we take up
the great themes
love pride hate envy
diagram the consequences
prove each to be superficial
leave the main characters
operating without motive
if i had to speak
i couldn't

Rob Patton was born in Chicago in 1943. He received the MFA from Cornell in 1970, and currently teaches creative writing there. This is his first published book.

....

Other books in the Ithaca House poetry series:

Stuart Peterfreund--THE HANGED KNIFE & OTHER POEMS

Stephen Shrader--LEAVING BY THE CLOSET DOOR

Frederick Buell--THESEUS & OTHER POEMS

Robert Allen--VALHALLA AT THE OK

all $2.95

Raymond DiPalma--THE GALLERY GOERS $1.50

Ronald Silliman--CROW $1.95

Forthcoming:

Karen Hanson--SPINE

Joseph Bruchac--INDIAN MOUNTAIN

Peter Wild--PELIGROS

Ralph Salisbury--THE GHOST GRAPEFRUIT & OTHER POEMS

David McAleavey--HEIRESS

Greg Kuzma--SONG FOR SOMEONE GOING AWAY

all $2.95

David Melnick--ECLOGS $1.95

Orders for any of these may be placed at:

ITHACA HOUSE

314 FOREST HOME DRIVE, ITHACA, NEW YORK 14850

$2.95

RLDS MOST

UTIFUL GIRLS

an Ithaca House book